T-Lloyd

In the Trenches

By Ron Berman
& Stephen McFadden

T-Lloyd: In the Trenches
COPYRIGHT 2008
by Ron Berman & Stephen McFadden

Scobre Press Corporation
2255 Calle Clara
La Jolla, CA 92037

Scobre Press books may be purchased for educational,
business or sales promotional use.
First Scobre edition published 2008.

Edited by Jenelle Nelson
Cover Art & Layout by Michael Lynch
Content Editing & Research by Arica Rai Zimmerman
Photos on pages 1, 40, 52, 53 & 56, by Ron Christopher
Photos on pages 31, 32, 37, 48, 49 & 59 by Brandon
Thibodeaux, **www.eye4light.com**

ISBN # 1-934713-20-1

TOUCHDOWN EDITION
This story is based on the real life of Thomas
Lloyd III, although some names, quotes, and
details of events have been altered.

CHAPTER ONE

THE LINE

Everything is quiet on the line. Almost *too* quiet. The sounds of the crowd seem far off in the distance. The players up front—the guys who look superhuman in size and strength—kneel across from one another in a 3-point stance. Hands clench into fists, cleats dig into the dirt, and hearts begin to race. In a few seconds, the ball will be hiked. Then the quiet calm will disappear, and the field will turn into a war zone, ruled by brute strength, strategy, athleticism, and passion.

Coaches bark last-minute instructions from the sidelines, but at this point they don't mean much to the guys on the line. Everybody knows what to do. Each player stares into the eyes of the person he will soon be doing battle with. There are just a few inches separating them, so a grunt, or even some trash talk, will be the last noise he hears before impact. For now, the only thing each player can do is wait behind the line and try not to flinch or show weakness.

The imaginary line that keeps these warriors apart is called the line of scrimmage. It's where every play begins, and where the outcome of every play is decided. The line can't be crossed by either team until the ball is hiked. This area is known to football players as the trenches. On both sides of the line are some of the strongest men on the planet—offensive and defensive linemen. From the start of the game until the very last play, this is where they earn their living and make names for themselves.

The action in the trenches is not pretty, and it's certainly not glamorous. Linemen are trained to hit hard and show no mercy. They want to strike quickly and with great force. Success is achieved when their opponents are lying face down on the field, unaware of anything except the smell of the dirt and grass stuck in their helmets.

The intense activity on the line sets the stage for everything else that happens in a football game: for the quarterback who leads his team into enemy territory, for the running back who explodes into the open field, and for the wide receiver who sprints past the defense and gracefully catches a pass for a touchdown.

Football holds a very special place in the hearts of countless Americans. Millions of fans tune in every Sunday from September to February to see how the season will play out for their favorite teams. The Super Bowl is the most anticipated sporting event of the year. It's watched by more than 130 million people from around the world.

Super Bowl tickets can sell for thousands of dollars each. This lucky fan got his hands on 6 tickets for Super Bowl XLII in Arizona (Giants vs. Patriots).

Across the nation, young football players are training hard and developing their skills every day. When summer ends and fall arrives, Friday nights mean one thing: high school football. From small towns in Pennsylvania and South Dakota, to large cities in California and Texas, epic battles take place on the gridiron. For these high school players, it's all about the love of the game. For many of them, it's also about trying to earn a college scholarship.

College is a whole different level, of course. To begin with, the players are bigger, faster, and stronger. That's also the time when many star players start thinking about making it in the pros. Sure, they've been dreaming about it their whole lives, but now it's so close they can almost taste it. They know how tough it is, though: less than 300 players are drafted into the NFL every year. It's a long shot, but still, most elite college football players wake up every day with that goal in mind.

The NFL draft, held in New York City every year since 1965, is exciting for both NFL hopefuls and fans watching the action at home. Pictured above, reporters anxiously await the Chicago Bears decision on their first round pick.

Aside from actually playing football, nothing is more exciting than watching a game in person. Most fans, when they can't attend a game, watch it on TV and cheer for their favorite teams. Yet, without realizing it, even the most knowledgeable football fan tends to focus only on the most obvious parts of the game. That's because the cameras follow the ball (for the most part). It's important to keep in mind that there are 22 players on the field at all times. So, following the ball the entire time gives viewers a limited idea of what is actually happening—especially in the trenches.

When the camera follows the ball, everyone else becomes a blur in the background.

When a play ends, the cameras often shift to the quarterback. We see his disappointment when he throws an interception or the satisfaction on his face when he tosses a pass for an important first down. But the quarterback isn't doing it all by himself. Most people don't realize just how much he depends on his teammates. His receivers have to find ways to get open. The offensive line has to block oncoming defenders to give him time to throw. His running backs have to recognize holes in the defense, and also help block on passing plays. If anyone doesn't do his job, the entire play breaks down.

To win a football game, an all-around team effort is required. There are 53 players on each NFL roster—far more than teams in other major sports—and any one of them might play a big role in the outcome of the game. In fact, during a 60-minute NFL game, most of these players will see action at some point.

Offensive teamwork all starts in the huddle. The players gather around the quarterback, who calls a play. The responsibility of the offensive linemen is to give him enough protection so he can execute that play. On the other side of the ball, the defensive line gets ready. They want to pressure the quarterback, while creating a wall of bodies that running backs can't penetrate. The next time you watch a football game in person, try an experiment: Don't watch the ball for a few plays—instead, focus on the action that is taking place at the line of scrimmage.

Even if the average fan doesn't pay much attention to the activity in the trenches, coaches and star football players certainly do. In 1991, Emmitt Smith of the Dallas Cowboys rushed for 1,563 yards. His response? He bought $5,000 Rolex watches for *each* player on his offensive line! He knew that without their skilled blocking, he wouldn't have had such a successful season. A running back makes his living running through holes created for him by his offensive line. As one prominent offensive coordinator says, "The line is the key—because if you can't protect the quarterback and run the ball, the game is lost."

For every offensive player who is trying to make the play run smoothly, there is a defensive player who is trying to disrupt it. For the most part, the cornerbacks and safeties are guarding the receivers. The linebackers are usually positioned between the linemen and the safeties and corners. Linebackers follow the ball—if it's a running play, they attack the line of scrimmage, looking to make a tackle. If it's a passing play, they either blitz the quarterback or drop back into coverage.

Defensive linemen are different. They are trying to plug the holes in the line and keep the offensive lineman from pushing them backward. Of course, if they get the chance, they will go after the quarterback or the running back. But that's not their main focus. They are simply trying to keep the line from moving ... and the other team from advancing forward.

That's what defense is all about—trying to *stop* skilled players like Tony Romo, Adrian Peterson, and Larry Fitzgerald. It's a difficult task, but the defensive mindset is to prevent these superstars from "doing their thing." Just ask any coach in the NFL, and he'll tell you that defense wins championships.

At right is the prestigious Vince Lombardi trophy, awarded each year to the winner of the Super Bowl. The award had originally been named the "World Championship Game Trophy." It was later renamed in honor of Coach Lombardi.

Speaking of defensive linemen, here's a quiz: think of your favorite NFL team and see if you can name the nose tackle. Stumped? Well, you're not the only one. Most football fans couldn't tell you who their nose tackle is. But football insiders know that he is one of the most important players on the field. The nose tackle, also sometimes called the nose guard, is the defensive lineman that lines up right on the *nose* of the football, across from the center. He's right there in the heart of the trenches.

When the ball is snapped, one, two, or sometimes even three blockers crash into the nose tackle—on *every* play. He must hold his ground so his teammates can make a play. This is why many coaches consider the nose tackle to be the anchor of the defense. If he is getting pushed backward, the offense is probably having a big day. On the other hand, if more than one offensive lineman has to worry about blocking the nose, that's one less guy available to protect the quarterback or open holes for the running back.

The job requirement for a nose tackle is simple: be willing to accept the punishment, and keep coming back for more—just so other guys can get the glory. Strap on your helmet, get out there, and get *pounded* ... on every play! That's the life of a nose tackle. Although it's not a glamorous position, it is manned by some of the strongest and bravest football players in the world. Bob Golic, a former all-pro nose tackle, might have said it best: "If you're mad at your kid, you can either raise him to be a nose tackle—or send him out to play on the *freeway*. It's about the same."

Golic's funny remark drives the point home very well. Nose tackles take an insane amount of pounding throughout the course of a football game. So, the obvious question is: Why on earth would anyone *want* to play this position? Well, one incredible young athlete might be able to provide the answer. His name is Thomas Lloyd III, known to his family as "T.J." With his friends, though, and on the football field, he goes by "T-Lloyd."

This 18-year-old nose tackle from Hurst, Texas—formerly of New Orleans—has loved the sport of football his entire life. But he wasn't born to play quarterback or wide receiver. He was built to be a warrior in the trenches. He's a team player who never gives up—and at about 270 pounds, he's a physically dominating force.

Vince Lombardi, perhaps the greatest coach in the history of professional football, once said, "Individual commitment to a group effort—that is what makes a team work, a company work, a society work, a civilization work." Nobody understands this idea better than nose tackles. One of the best of them is Thomas Lloyd III—T-Lloyd.

T-Lloyd (in the white shirt and white hat) poses with some of his teammates.

CHAPTER TWO

ROUGH BEGINNING

"It's just not fair," little Thomas said, trying to hold back the tears. Actually, "little" was probably not an accurate description of 10-year-old Thomas Lloyd III. He was anything *but* little. As a matter of fact, that was the problem. That's why the officials of the Pop Warner league wouldn't let him play. The weight limit was 135 pounds, but Thomas tipped the scale at 160 pounds. He wasn't unhealthy; he was simply a big kid.

The other boys seemed relieved. None of them wanted to go head-to-head with Thomas. When he left the field that day with his father, Thomas was really upset that he hadn't been allowed to participate. It was a pretty big blow to a kid who had wanted to play football ever since he could remember.

Growing up in Violet, a small town just outside of New Orleans, Thomas Lloyd III was glued to the TV every weekend, watching football. "T.J.," as his family called him, was completely obsessed with the game. He watched college football on Saturday and pro games on Sunday. As a proud resident of the state of Louisiana, he rooted for the LSU (Louisiana State University) Tigers and the New Orleans Saints.

T-Lloyd never stopped rooting for the Tigers.

Thomas couldn't get enough of football. His dad, a former high school linebacker, explained the game to his oldest son in great detail. From the very beginning, Thomas was fascinated by the line of scrimmage and the one-on-one battles that shaped the outcome of games. He learned to appreciate how each player tries to do his part to help the team win.

After being excluded from Pop Warner, the next couple of weeks were tough on Thomas—that is, until he passed by some older kids in the neighborhood who were playing a pick-up football game. He walked up to them and asked if he could play. Although he was a few years younger, he was still one of the biggest kids out there. Thomas started playing with them all the time. If he couldn't be on a real team, this was the next best thing.

Although pick-up football was fun, it wasn't a structured environment like Pop Warner. This youth football league, which has been around for almost 80 years, provides excellent coaching for a quarter of a million kids each year. And coaching was exactly what Thomas needed. He desperately wanted to become a better player. Pick-up games with no pads and no linemen were fun, but they did little to prepare Thomas for the real thing.

Luckily, Thomas' dad was there for him. Even though Mr. Lloyd was busy with work, he always found time to teach his son the basics of football. They practiced many things, such as getting into a three-point stance, and how to fight off blockers.

The lessons continued over the next couple of years. One night, when Mr. Lloyd came into Thomas' bedroom to say goodnight, he found his son in pajamas, still wearing his New Orleans Saints kid-sized helmet. Thomas was standing in the middle of the room, practicing lining up on the offensive line, something they had been working on recently.

Looking up, Thomas smiled. "Remember how they didn't let me play on Pop Warner a few years ago? Well, I don't care about that anymore—'cause I'll be ready once middle school starts. Nobody's gonna stop me from making the team."

Mr. Lloyd laughed. He was proud that his son was so determined. He was glad to see that Thomas had bounced back from the disappointment of missing out on Pop Warner.

When Thomas enrolled at PGT Beauregard Middle School, he definitely felt that he was ready. He had worked hard, improving his quickness, lateral movement, and overall fitness. By now he weighed a solid 220 pounds. When he wasn't playing or practicing, he was studying the moves of great linemen on TV. All Thomas could think about was becoming a member of his middle school football team.

It's usually tough going to a new school and meeting new people. Not for Thomas. He is friendly and outgoing, so he made new friends and fit in without much trouble.

But he was in for a shock when he showed up at football tryouts. Middle school was a whole new level. He wasn't the only kid who had been improving his skills on the football field. To make it even more challenging, Thomas was only a sixth grader, while most of the other players were seventh or eighth graders. They were older, more experienced, and in a better position to earn a spot on the team.

It turned out to be a rough beginning for Thomas, who hadn't played much organized football up to that point. Even the drills the coaches ran were new to him. He had never even participated in a basic "2 on 1" drill. This punishing drill is all about trying to split a double team. Two players line up and block a single player, whose job is to hold his ground—or, even better, fight through them so he can reach the quarterback or running back. It's not a complicated drill, but it was tiring and difficult for someone who had never done it before.

Between long practices, new drills, and complicated plays, Thomas definitely struggled. But he never became frustrated. It was clear that he had two things that nobody could match: heart and determination. The coaches picked up on it, especially when they noticed him getting knocked down repeatedly, but quickly getting up. At one point, an assistant coach took pity and offered Thomas a water break. Shaking his head and popping right back to his feet, Thomas refused.

This work ethic paid off when Thomas became an official member of the PGT Beauregard "Generals." Of course, making the team was one thing, but getting playing time was another. Week after week, he watched from the sidelines. Even though he busted his butt in practice, the coaches were going with the older kids.

It was late in the season when Thomas finally saw some action. The Generals were ahead 21-6 with five minutes remaining in the game. This blow-out meant that the starters could get some much-needed rest. The coach looked over at Thomas and yelled, "Get in there, Grunt!" (Grunt is a term that refers to a lineman.)

Snapping on his chinstrap, Thomas sprinted onto the field and took his spot on the defensive line. His eyes focused on the ball as he waited anxiously for the center to make the snap. As soon as that happened, Thomas drove forward like a runaway truck, colliding with two huge offensive linemen. Like a man possessed, he used a surge of power to force his way between the blockers and grab the quarterback, throwing him to the turf. Amazingly, Thomas had sacked the quarterback on his first play ever!

This was the beginning of a promising career for a talented young athlete. Yet, looking back on his first game, Thomas laughs, "I had no clue what I was doing out there. I was just so excited to be on the field. I don't know if that first play was luck, skill, or just pure adrenalin. Either way, it really set the tone for the rest of my career."

That play was only the beginning. Thomas soon earned a starting spot on the defensive line. Over the course of his middle school career, he showed significant improvement week after week.

By the time he graduated from middle school, Thomas Lloyd III had become a different player. He even earned a nickname: "T-Lloyd." He was eagerly looking forward to entering high school the following year. St. Bernard had an excellent football program, so making his mark there would be tough. T-Lloyd realized that it might take a year or two, but he felt that eventually he would develop into a solid varsity player. He truly believed that nothing could stop him from having a rewarding high school football career in the great state of Louisiana.

CHAPTER THREE

THE STORM

One year later, when the bell rang on the final day of the school year, everybody in T-Lloyd's class cheered. As for T-Lloyd, he couldn't wipe the grin off his face. It was June of 2005. He had just completed his freshman year of high school, and he had never been happier. As people started streaming out of St. Bernard High to begin summer vacation, T-Lloyd had no doubt that it was going to be one of the best summers of his life.

What a year it had been. For the first time ever, T-Lloyd felt like a *real* football player. All the hard work and sacrifice had paid off. Incredibly, he had made the varsity ... as a freshman! Although he wasn't yet playing nose tackle—the position that would ultimately make him a high school star—he had become a skilled offensive lineman.

Just making varsity would have been enough for most freshmen, but T-Lloyd wasn't satisfied. From the very first day of practice, he gave 100% effort. Learning from his mistakes, he showed steady improvement. It was an amazing season in which he earned all-league honors.

That wasn't the only accolade T-Lloyd earned that year. He also took home the "Coach's Award." This award was given to the most respectful and hard-working player on the team. The honor reminded T-Lloyd that being successful in football takes commitment and dedication.

T-Lloyd has always gotten along with his coaches.

T-Lloyd was psyched about summer vacation. He was planning to kick back, spend time in the weight room, and hang out with his friends. As they walked out the front door of St. Bernard High School, T-Lloyd and his classmates signed each other's yearbooks under the hot Louisiana sun. Life seemed perfect at that moment.

A few months later, T-Lloyd was driving to the gym. Summer was a blast, living up to all his expectations. On this day, he was cruising along and feeling relaxed. The radio was blasting "On my Own," by Lil' Wayne, one of his favorite rappers. The bass shook the car as T-Lloyd rolled to the beat.

When T-Lloyd's cell phone beeped, indicating he had a text message, he thought nothing of it. He stopped at the next red light and glanced down at his phone. It was from his mom. "Did you hear about the storm?" she asked. "Come home as soon as you can."

It was Wednesday, August 24, 2005. T-Lloyd knew that his mom was talking about the reports that had been on TV the last couple of days. Apparently there was a huge storm headed to Florida's Gulf Coast, which is located in the southeastern part of the United States. Louisiana, where T-Lloyd and his family were living, is approximately 200 miles away from Florida. "Yeah, no big deal," he texted back. "I'll be home after the gym."

When T-Lloyd returned home later that day, the only new development was that the storm had been upgraded. It was now being called a tropical storm, which is more violent. It had even been given a name: *Katrina*. That name would soon be forever carved into the minds and hearts of Americans across the country.

The next day, Thursday, the tropical storm was upgraded yet again, this time to a hurricane—Hurricane *Katrina*. It had nearly doubled in strength and intensity. The actual definition of a hurricane is a powerful storm with very high, swirling winds. The dangerous winds of a hurricane can cause catastrophic destruction. The best defense against a hurricane is to leave the area as quickly as possible.

Naturally, all of these issues were a major topic of discussion in the Lloyd household. Louisiana is part of the Gulf Coast region of the United States—along with Florida, Texas, Mississippi, and Alabama. There was a strong possibility that the hurricane might make its way to them.

At first, there was no reason for the Lloyds or their neighbors to be overly concerned. The year before, a huge storm had been predicted to hit, so they all left. Yet, when they returned to their homes the next day, there had been no damage. "We figured it would be the same thing," T-Lloyd explains. "When the storm warnings came, we thought we were just going to leave for a little while and then come right back."

On Friday, August 26, T-Lloyd and his younger brother Tevin piled into the family car with their mom behind the wheel. They were headed to Dallas, Texas, which was a drive of about five hours. The plan was for them to stay with relatives, while Mr. Lloyd stayed behind to look after their house.

When Mrs. Lloyd and her sons hit the highway, they knew right away that something unusual was happening. The roads were jammed with cars desperate to get out of town. It was bumper-to-bumper the entire way to Dallas. A trip that should have taken five hours took almost *26* hours!

When they finally made it to their aunt's home, Mrs. Lloyd and her boys immediately turned on the television. They were horrified by the images they saw.

Katrina destroyed nearly everything in its path.

Most of New Orleans was flooded at this point. Even their high school, St. Bernard, was completely under water.

In the aftermath of Hurricane Katrina, New Orleans looked more like a river than a city.

The news was saying that Hurricane *Katrina* was one of the worst natural disasters ever to hit the United States—and Mr. Lloyd was still in the middle of it! To make matters worse, they couldn't reach him. Every call to his cell phone went straight to voicemail. T-Lloyd and his family started to pray. They prayed that Mr. Lloyd had managed to escape.

The next couple of days were a living nightmare. As each new detail was revealed, the fear increased. The news reported on the death and destruction caused by *Katrina,* and it seemed to be getting worse and worse. With every new image that popped up on the screen, T-Lloyd's heart sank. He feared for his neighbors, his friends—and most of all, for his father.

By Sunday, August 28, things seemed hopeless. That morning, the winds created by Hurricane *Katrina* reached speeds of close to 200 miles per hour. To show how insane that is, consider this: a NASCAR driver at the Daytona 500 can hit speeds of up to 200 miles per hour!

The worst part for the Lloyd family was the uncertainty. Almost everybody who was stranded in New Orleans was unable to communicate with the outside world. T-Lloyd hadn't heard anything from his dad in almost three days. Seeing horrible video footage on TV of dead bodies floating down the flooded streets was almost too much to bear. It was impossible not to wonder: was Mr. Lloyd one of those unfortunate souls?

There was a lot going on in T-Lloyd's heart during those confused hours and days. He couldn't stop thinking about his dad. In his mind, he replayed images of them talking, laughing, and watching football together. Sometimes the feelings of fear and grief were overwhelming.

Two days later, Tuesday, T-Lloyd was completely dejected. He couldn't take his eyes off the TV, even though watching just made things worse. It was one awful thing after another. People were dying, others were starving, houses had been destroyed, and nothing seemed to be getting better. *How can something like this be happening?* He wondered. Even though he didn't say anything to worry his mom or brother, T-Lloyd was losing hope.

And then the phone rang... T-Lloyd almost flew out of the chair he was sitting in. "Hello," he answered anxiously. The last week had been the worst of his entire life. After all that, was this phone call going to bring even more horrifying news? *Is my dad alive or not?* This was the question running through T-Lloyd's mind during the one second it took him to answer the telephone.

Hearing the phone ring, T-Lloyd's mom, his brother, and all their relatives had raced into the room. Now they were staring at T-Lloyd with faces of hope and terror, all rolled into one. T-Lloyd braced himself. Then, when he heard his father's voice on the other end of the line, it was the sweetest sound he could have ever imagined. Trying to hold back tears of joy, T-Lloyd yelled out, "Dad! You're okay!" Everyone started screaming. It was a moment that none of them would ever forget.

After celebrating for a few seconds, everyone crouched around the phone to hear Mr. Lloyd tell his amazing story of survival. When the hurricane hit, the streets immediately started flooding. Mr. Lloyd was in extreme danger. Thinking quickly, he managed to jump on a neighbor's car and hold on for dear life as it floated down the street!

That was just the beginning. From there, Mr. Lloyd made it on to the roof of a building, where he huddled with other survivors. There was very little water to drink, and nothing to eat. They were all wet, confused, and scared. But they refused to give up. For his part, Mr. Lloyd just kept thinking about his wife, T-Lloyd, and Tevin. He was determined to make his way back to them.

A few days later, Mr. Lloyd got a ride on a boat to a shelter where hundreds of other people were also stranded. He spent two more days there, until he was finally transported to an emergency shelter that was better equipped. Once there, he was able to get some food for the first time in five days. More importantly, somebody let him borrow a cell phone. As soon as he heard T-Lloyd's voice, Mr. Lloyd knew that his struggle had been worth it.

A couple of days later, Mr. Lloyd caught a flight to Dallas to join his family. He had a tearful reunion with Mrs. Lloyd, T-Lloyd, and Tevin at the airport.

Reunited.

At that moment, nothing mattered: not the pain and suffering, or even the aftermath of one of the worst hurricanes in the history of the United States. Still, decisions had to be made. Would the family be able to return home? Would T-Lloyd and Tevin be able to start school again in New Orleans?

T-Lloyd was so happy to see his dad that he didn't think about any of these things at first. Still, his future, which had looked so certain a few months earlier, was now completely up in the air. He had absolutely no idea what would happen next.

T-Lloyd ponders his future.

CHAPTER FOUR

FRIDAY NIGHT LIGHTS

Once in a while, T-Lloyd pulls out the plaque and looks at it—that simple wood plaque with the words "Coach's Award 2004" engraved on the front. It's the award he earned at the end of his freshman season at St. Bernard High School.

While T-Lloyd doesn't need honors or awards to get him pumped up, the Coach's Award plaque is significant for a different reason. It is one of the few items that his family managed to save after Hurricane *Katrina* hit New Orleans. Shrugging his massive shoulders, T-Lloyd reflects on everything that has happened since then. One minute he was preparing for his sophomore year at St. Bernard High School. Then Hurricane *Katrina* swept through and changed his life forever.

Several weeks after the storm disappeared, the Lloyds were finally able to return to their house—or what was left of it. Seeing their home in such a damaged state was gut-wrenching. Mr. Lloyd had to kick in the front door just to get inside, because the key didn't work.

The family walked in, only to see mud and water everywhere. Most of their possessions were ruined. The walls were falling apart. The furniture was destroyed. There was no way they could live in the house in its current state. So, with great sadness, Mr. and Mrs. Lloyd made the difficult but necessary decision to move.

As depressing as the situation was, the Lloyds knew that they were not alone. Thousands of families were affected by Hurricane *Katrina*. Close to 2,000 people died, and thousands of homes were damaged beyond repair. The financial loss was dramatic. According to some estimates, the storm was responsible for more than $81 *billion* worth of damage.

Like most families displaced by the hurricane, the Lloyds' first concern was finding a new place to live. With relatives in nearby Texas, moving there seemed like a logical choice. Luckily, Mr. and Mrs. Lloyd received some help from a government agency known as FEMA, which stands for Federal Emergency Management Agency. The role of this organization is to assist people during disasters like *Katrina*. With FEMA's help, the Lloyds found an apartment.

The next thing T-Lloyd knew, he was heading back to Texas. The Lloyds were used to traveling there to visit relatives. Now they were going there to live. Watching the miles disappear, T-Lloyd wondered what life would be like in the "Lone Star State."

As many people like to say, "Everything is bigger in Texas." In some ways this is really true. It's a huge state, with a population of more than 20 million people. Driving from one end of the state to the other would take well over ten hours. Another thing that's huge in Texas is sports. It's such a big state that it has two NFL teams, two Major League baseball teams, and *three* NBA teams.

Although the circumstances under which T-Lloyd left New Orleans were sad, at least he was able to feel some excitement about moving to a state that is so enthusiastic about sports—especially high school football. There is no doubt that Texans take a lot of pride in it. On Friday nights in the late summer and fall, there's no better place to be than the local high school football field. In cities and towns all across Texas, it's normal to have as many as 10,000 fans pack the stands to support their local team!

America got an up close and personal look at Texas high school football in H. G. Bissinger's famous book, "Friday Night Lights," which was later turned into a movie and hit TV show. The book is about a small town and its obsession with the local high school football team. It makes an important point: In Texas, high school football is more than a sport ... it's almost like a religion.

T-Lloyd was aware of all this. He knew he would miss his friends back in Louisiana, but he also realized that he had a great opportunity. When it comes to football, Texas is a very important state. As a matter of fact, along with California and Florida, it has produced the most NFL players. The bottom line is that if you're good in Texas, *everybody* knows about it. There are newspaper articles, magazines, and cable shows—not to mention college scouts all over the place.

The Lloyds settled in a small city called Hurst. It's never easy to start over and enroll in a new school, but both T-Lloyd and Tevin stayed positive. When T-Lloyd had his first chance to look around the campus of Hurst L.D. Bell High School, he was impressed. The weight room, stadium, and even the locker room were all incredible! It seemed like everything at Bell was twice the size of St. Bernard.

T-Lloyd quickly got in the swing of life in Hurst. With his upbeat, laid-back attitude, he became popular right away. The fact that he was a football player made it even easier.

The transition to Texas football was not quite as simple. T-Lloyd knew he was going to have to make some major adjustments. The competition in Texas was better than what he had seen back in Louisiana. Plus, he would need to adjust to the pressure of playing in front of huge crowds. The entire town of Hurst followed the action of their beloved "Blue Raiders" every Friday night. Hundreds of loyal fans even traveled on the road with the team.

When T-Lloyd met Coach Gary Olivo, the head coach at Bell, things got a little easier. Coach Olivo saw something in T-Lloyd right away. By the end of the 2005 season, T-Lloyd was a starting offensive lineman on the junior varsity squad. Coach Olivo had no doubt that by the following season, T-Lloyd would be a varsity player. Things had happened quickly, because this was less than six months since the disaster of Hurricane *Katrina*.

The other members of the Blue Raiders welcomed T-Lloyd with open arms. They noticed how hard he worked on every play, which helped him earn their respect. Being part of a football team is a unique experience. More often than not, players become great friends on and off the field. Because everyone has to depend so much on each other, a special bond is created.

DeAnte Piper, a talented running back, quickly became T-Lloyd's closest friend on the team. But T-Lloyd is quick to point out, "*All* the guys on the team are like family. They accepted me from day one. We're all tight." Laughing, he adds, "They love coming over to my house for my mom's famous jambalaya. They've found out that the best food comes from Louisiana."

T-Lloyd's Mom serves up some of her homemade jambalaya, which is a Louisiana Creole dish of Spanish and French creation.

T-Lloyd's sophomore year was a success. Sure, there was still an aching in his heart about St. Bernard High, and the good life he had been forced to leave behind in New Orleans. But there was no point looking back.

By the time that first season ended, T-Lloyd had blended in well and adjusted to his new life. New Orleans would always be a part of him—but he was a Texan now, and ready for bigger and better things on the football field.

Making friends has never been a problem for an outgoing guy like T-Lloyd. Here, he plays with his new iPhone while DeAnte watches a Brett Favre press conference on TV.

CHAPTER FIVE

NEW POSITION

T-Lloyd enjoyed a relaxed and easygoing summer in 2006. After the trauma of Hurricane *Katrina*, and the difficulty of moving to a new state and to a new school, it was nice to have some down time.

Of course, the one thing T-Lloyd was most looking forward to was the start of football season—and trying to earn a spot on the varsity squad. As a matter of fact, he had begun preparing for that challenge right after the conclusion of his sophomore season. At that time, Coach Olivo and the assistant coaches had taken him aside and given him some news that would alter the course of his career.

Coach Olivo had made an important decision. He wanted T-Lloyd to learn a new position. He talked to T-Lloyd about moving back to the *defensive* line, where T-Lloyd had played in middle school. In the opinion of all the coaches, the position that would fit his game best was nose tackle. They felt that T-Lloyd's combination of size and strength made him the perfect choice to play this demanding position.

This wasn't a decision Coach Olivo and his assistants had made randomly. They had given it a lot of thought. Football is truly an amazing game. On one hand, it's a ferocious street fight. On the other hand, it's a delicate battle of strategy and field position. Coaches are constantly moving players and shifting strategies in an effort to gain an advantage. There are dozens of different offensive and defensive schemes.

Take the "3-4" defense, for example. This is a defensive scheme in which three linemen play in front of four linebackers.

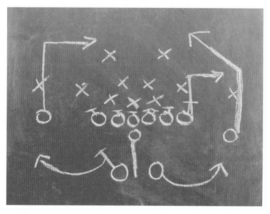

In the diagram above, the "X's" represent defensive players. The "O's" represent offensive players. The 3 "X's" directly across from the group of 6 "O's" are the defensive linemen. The "X" in the middle of those 3 "X's" is the nose tackle.

This formation makes it tougher for the offense to block the linebackers, due to the fact that there are so many of them—and the offense never knows which of them are going to rush. Most teams can't play a 3-4 because without that extra lineman in the trenches, they have a hard time stopping their opponent's running game. The best way to make a 3-4 defense work is to have a big and skilled nose tackle.

When the ball is snapped, the job of the nose tackle is to "eat up" the blockers assigned to him. (Eating up players means staying on them and keeping them busy so they aren't able to block other players.) It's one of the toughest jobs in football because a nose tackle playing in the 3-4 usually has to eat up two, and sometimes even three players at a time. This allows speedy linebackers to guard the pass *and* the run more effectively.

Choosing defensive schemes is crucial, and can have a huge impact on the success or failure of a team. As any good football coach will tell you, it comes down to the personnel he has to work with. If a coach has athletic linebackers and a few big, hulking linemen, he might be inclined to play a 3-4. Most teams usually go with the traditional 4-3 scheme, though, with four big linemen and three speedy linebackers. This is the most balanced defense for guarding against the pass and the rush.

Game strategy and shifting defensive formations is what led to Coach Olivo's idea to move T-Lloyd to nose tackle. He wanted to start playing the non-traditional 3-4 defense. First, though, he needed an anchor on the line—a guy who was so big and strong, and so tough, that having him in the trenches was almost like having *two* players there. Having seen T-Lloyd's ability and never-quit attitude, the coach came to the conclusion that he could be the focus of a new and improved defense with a 3-4 formation.

For T-Lloyd, this opportunity seemed perfect. As soon as the coaches gave him the news, it was like a light bulb went off in his head. He had always been interested in playing defense anyway. Plus, he realized that switching to nose tackle might be a good career move. Like many young football players, he dreams that one day he'll be playing in the NFL.

To understand just how difficult it is to get to the NFL, consider this: there are about 13,000 college seniors who are football players. The NFL draft consists of seven rounds, and there are 32 teams in the league. This means that only 1 out of 50 (for a total of approximately 250 players) will get drafted.

Of course, the rewards are tremendous ... *if* you get there. In 2006, the New Orleans Saints drafted USC star running back Reggie Bush with the second pick overall. They promptly signed him to a six-year, $54 million deal.

Even players who go near the bottom of the NFL draft sign large contracts. Marques Colston was the 252nd pick in that same draft. That was only five picks away from not being drafted at all. Colston was a virtually unknown wide receiver from Hofstra University. Still, he signed a three-year deal with the Saints worth just under a million dollars. Not bad for a player who nearly went undrafted!

Here's the interesting part, though. While most fans expected Reggie Bush to be an instant superstar, nobody gave a second thought to Marques Colston. But in the Saints' first game of the season, he started at wide receiver and caught a touchdown pass! Colston went to on to have a spectacular season, almost winning the Rookie of the Year award. His story is a reminder to young football players that if they work hard, it's not impossible to get drafted and even become a great NFL player.

Nobody understands this better than T-Lloyd. That's why he was so enthusiastic about switching to nose tackle. Without question, it would be a tough challenge. If he excelled, however, he would have a better chance of being an NFL draft pick someday. This is because nose tackle is a specialty position. While there are tons of quarterbacks, wide receivers, and linebackers, not many people have the size and skill to be a good nose tackle.

T-Lloyd's junior year of high school began with the challenge of learning his new role. It wasn't easy, but he was determined to succeed. Luckily, he had help every step of the way.

Defensive coordinator Andy Modica had already spent a lot of time with T-Lloyd, teaching him various defensive schemes. Now that practice was starting up, T-Lloyd showed up early every day to study the basics of playing nose tackle. It didn't take long for Coach Olivo to realize that it had been a great decision. T-Lloyd took to the position quickly.

Still, it was one thing to practice on the field when the stands were empty. But playing a game in front of 8,000 screaming fans would be completely different. Yet, strangely, before the first game of the season, T-Lloyd wasn't nervous. He had been waiting for a moment like this his entire life.

At Bell, nothing can match the excitement of running onto the field right before the game starts—especially the first game of the year. The varsity players stand under a canopy at the front of the field. Everyone gathers around the captains; their job is to lead the team onto the field. Then, when the announcer gives the signal, the players come charging out toward the middle of the field. The fans go wild, as flash bulbs from cameras all around the stadium light up the Friday night sky.

When T-Lloyd experienced this moment, he knew it would remain in his heart and mind forever. There was nothing like playing in front of a big Texas crowd.

T-Lloyd's junior season was a great success. He flourished in his new position and soon became one of the leaders on the defensive line. The new 3-4 defensive scheme worked well, too. The Blue Raiders soon became known throughout the region as a ferocious defensive team.

By the last game of the season, T-Lloyd was already looking forward to next year, when he would be a senior. He had come to the conclusion that he needed to get even bigger and stronger. He had learned that nothing is more important for a nose tackle.

T-Lloyd knew exactly what he needed to do. He didn't want to waste a minute, so as soon as the season ended, he went straight to work.

CHAPTER SIX

PUMPING IRON

When T-Lloyd had attended St. Bernard High in New Orleans, he had lifted weights, but not intensely. But everything changed once he became a nose tackle. To be effective at his new position, he would need to add some extra bulk and take his conditioning to an entirely new level.

Luckily, Bell had an excellent weightlifting program. The coaches and trainers designed a custom workout for T-Lloyd. He was enthusiastic about it, but he hadn't realized what a commitment it would be. At first he had to force himself to wake up early every day for weightlifting sessions before school. Soon, though, he looked forward to his alarm clock ringing before the sun came up. After just a couple weeks of pumping iron, T-Lloyd was hooked.

The coaches were amazed by T-Lloyd's physical transformation. He went from big and strong, to *huge*, in a short amount of time. Soon T-Lloyd was one of the strongest members of the team—able to match anyone on the bench press and the squat.

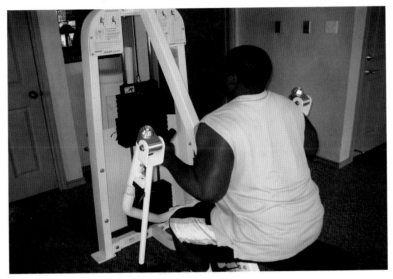

When it comes to size and strength, everyone is *not* created equal. It's not just how hard you work in the weight room, either. Some people are just naturally strong. T-Lloyd is definitely one of those people. Still, it took a lot of time and effort to develop his body and fulfill his potential.

That's exactly what Larry Allen did. Some people regard Allen as the strongest player in NFL history. Like T-Lloyd, Allen was always naturally strong, but his dedication and hard work in the weight room separated him from his peers. At 6-feet-3-inches and 325 pounds, the Dallas Cowboys standout was one of the best offensive linemen ever. His legendary status was earned in the weight room, however, not on the football field. By most standards, it's impressive to bench a weight that is equal to the amount of your entire body. In Allen's case, he benched more than *double* his body weight—nearly 700 pounds!

Although T-Lloyd wasn't quite at that level, he maintained his routine in the weight room, getting stronger and stronger. Over time, he started to enjoy lifting weights almost as much as playing football. This is not unusual among nose tackles, or football players in general. The giants who roam the defensive and offensive lines of football squads across the nation must possess a passion for weightlifting. After all, it is as much a part of their lives as eating, breathing, sleeping—and playing football, of course.

One aspect of weightlifting that appeals to T-Lloyd is the progress you make. It's pretty simple: The more weight you're able to lift, the stronger you're getting. It's easy to keep track of your improvement because weightlifters usually write down the amount of weight they lift. That way, every couple of weeks they can try to add some extra weight. For T-Lloyd, there's no more satisfying feeling than loading a couple of additional plates on the bar.

This type of training is not a perfectly smooth ride, though. Anyone that lifts weights knows that there are stretches of time when you feel stuck, unable to increase the amount you're lifting. Although it's natural, it can be frustrating. T-Lloyd was determined not to let this happen to him. But, as with all weightlifters, it did.

Even the strongest guys can get frustrated.

One day, T-Lloyd was at the Bell High gym in a bad mood. He was tired, and unable to push through the set. The weight room was empty except for one other kid who T-Lloyd recognized from around school. He had heard someone say that his name was ... wait, to protect his identity, let's just call him "Robbie." T-Lloyd figured that Robbie was probably on the baseball or wrestling team, because there was no arguing that he was ripped. Robbie noticed T-Lloyd struggling—breathing hard and muttering under his breath. Stepping away from a squat machine, Robbie approached T-Lloyd.

"What's up, T-Lloyd? You all right?" he asked.

"Yeah, man," T-Lloyd gave him a strange look, unsure of why this guy was approaching him. "I'm cool, thanks, just going through a rough patch. I can't get over the hump on the bench."

"I've been there," Robbie said. Then he took a few steps closer to T-Lloyd and looked around the room to make sure nobody was around. "You need to get with the program. How else you figure on playing college ball?" He reached into his backpack, "I got the prescription."

Robbie was certainly no doctor. T-Lloyd knew exactly what "prescription" he was talking about: steroids. Although T-Lloyd had only been lifting seriously for a couple of months, he knew all about steroids. He had seen people on TV and on the Internet discussing it. Even his parents and coaches had warned him about the dangers of steroids.

A lot of people don't even know what steroids are. Very simply, they are synthetic male hormones—meaning they act like male hormones, which exist naturally in the body. But when you take steroids, the amount of male hormones in your body becomes dangerously high and *unnatural.*

Male hormones are responsible for the development of a boy's body: puberty, muscle growth, and other male sexual characteristics. The problem is that when you mess with the levels of these hormones in your body (by taking steroids), weird and disastrous results occur. For example, taking steroids can shrink your testicles, make you go bald, and even cause you to develop breasts. They have also been linked to some forms of cancer. What guy wants any of *those* things?

Steroids can be taken in the form of pills, liquid, gel, or cream. They can also be injected. They're not new. In fact, they've been around for more than 100 years. During the 1930s, German scientists worked to develop synthetic testosterone, a form of steroids. They actually won the Nobel Prize for Chemistry for their efforts.

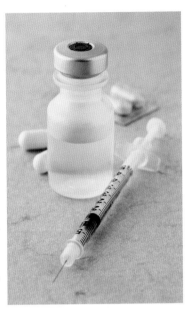

In 1945, the Germans gave steroids to prisoners of war to test the effects. Just a couple of years later, word got out about the effectiveness of steroids for weightlifters. Athletes around the world began using them to prepare for Olympic competitions. Because of their damaging side effects and the illegal advantage they give to athletes, steroids were banned from the Olympics. They are now also banned for athletes in every major sport.

Of course, that hasn't stopped some pro athletes from using them. This was confirmed in the "Mitchell Report." In 2007, former Senator George Mitchell was hired by Major League Baseball to investigate steroid use in professional baseball.

His conclusion was stunning: Senator Mitchell pointed to 80 baseball players who, according to the Senator, had taken "performance enhancing drugs." However, he made it clear that this was just the tip of the iceberg. His report suggested that a staggering number of Major Leaguers had also possibly taken steroids at some point.

Through the years, there has always been a temptation for high school athletes to take steroids to get ahead. They want to build up muscle quickly so they can perform at a higher level on the football field, baseball diamond, or basketball court. They've heard the whispering about college and pro athletes doing it. But, as T-Lloyd knows, the side effects of steroids are no joke. Plus, if you ever test positive, you can kiss any chance of a college scholarship goodbye.

"What do you think?" Robbie looked at T-Lloyd with a sly smile, revealing the bottle of pills in his hand. "I can give you the first dose free—just to try it out." To his surprise, the giant football player shook his head.

"You need to get that stuff away from me before you and me have a problem, man." Then T-Lloyd stood up, hovering over Robbie with the same intimidating look he gave to opposing lineman. "Right now," he said.

"Okay, man, take it easy," Robbie tossed the pills back in his bag, and quickly walked away with a scared look on his face.

T-Lloyd got back to his workout, grunting twice as hard as he pushed through his final set.

If former NFL great Lyle Alzado had been there at that moment, he would have applauded T-Lloyd for the way he dealt with Robbie. Alzado was a fierce all-pro defensive player who was a superstar in the 1970s and 1980s. Unfortunately, as he later admitted, he was also a steroids user. Sadly, Alzado died from a brain tumor at age 43. Many people believe his death was the result of taking steroids.

If you use steroids, you are risking everything . Is it worth it?

There will always be people who try to beat the system. Some will cheat on tests instead of studying, or steal money instead of earning it. In sports, some will take steroids instead of just working as hard as possible in a natural way. People who cheat always look for an edge, trying to stay one step ahead.

In life, however, there are consequences for every action. If you cheat on a test, you'll be given an "F" and possibly even get suspended. If you get caught stealing, you can go to jail. And, as Lyle Alzado would have told Robbie, if you use steroids you're risking your life.

After several scandals, all professional sports leagues have made a commitment to drug-free competition. There's nothing more exciting and pure than sports and competition. Nobody should have

47

an unfair advantage, especially if it involves jeopardizing the health of athletes.

After continuing his weightlifting program for the rest of the school year and then the summer, T-Lloyd felt better than ever before. He was going to be a senior, which meant that college wasn't far off. This was a great motivation for him. He knew that he would need to have a solid season to attract college scouts—and he was ready to do exactly that.

From early on, T-Lloyd's parents had instilled two things in him: the love of football and the tremendous benefits of a college education. They had worked hard their entire lives, just to give their two sons every possible advantage. For T-Lloyd, a college education would open many doors for him, in football and beyond.

But after the devastation of *Katrina*, which caused their home to be practically destroyed, paying for college would be difficult for Mr. and Mrs. Lloyd. T-Lloyd was aware that if he could earn a college scholarship, it would be the greatest gift he could ever give to his parents—and to himself.

CHAPTER SEVEN

BIG GAME

"I don't have to tell you guys how important this game is," Coach Olivo said, staring into the eyes of the players gathered around him. "Go out there and win it for yourselves, for your friends, for your family—and win it for Bell!"

The players strapped on their helmets and ran out of the locker room. As T-Lloyd made his way onto the field, he was as ready as he had ever been. This game meant so much ... a chance for Bell to get to the playoffs and possibly compete for the state title. As the Blue Raiders made their way onto the field, the crowd of 8,000 excited fans exploded with cheers.

Not only was this a chance to clinch a spot in the postseason, but it was also a bounce-back game. Bell had been crushed a week earlier by Irving Macarthur, one of the best teams in the district, 35-21. It was a severe blow to the Blue Raiders, because a win would have put them in a position to win the District 7-5A title for the first time in several years.

This game was their shot at redemption. Unfortunately, the Blue Raiders had to face another tough opponent, the South Grand Prairie "Warriors." To add to the drama, the Warriors had whipped them 35-6 the previous year. T-Lloyd would never forget that game, and not just because of the beat down—but also because he had sprained his ankle on the *very first play* of the game. It was a bad sprain that caused his ankle to swell up like a grapefruit. T-Lloyd wasn't able to play the rest of that game. Today was going to be payback time ... hopefully.

The game was a tense struggle. After three quarters, South Grand Prairie led 14-8. T-Lloyd and his teammates on the defensive line were playing a solid game. But their opponents were playing great defense, too. As hard as Bell tried, they couldn't get much of anything going on the offensive end. T-Lloyd had no control over that, of course. All the defense could do was try to shut the Warriors down and keep the score close.

In the fourth quarter, T-Lloyd was at his best. At times it felt like he was taking on the entire offensive line. They were throwing two, and sometimes three offensive linemen at him. He met the challenge head on, fighting through the pressure and giving his teammates the opportunity to make big plays defensively.

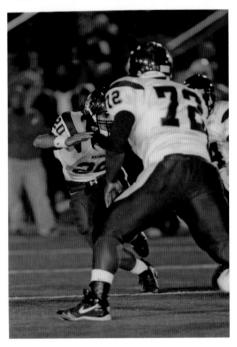

Offensively, though, Bell was still struggling. As each second ticked off the clock, they became more and more desperate. Soon there were only two minutes left in the game! The situation seemed hopeless, especially when the Warriors managed to get down to Bell's 30-yard line. They had the ball and the lead, with the clock ticking away. A few yards closer and they would be able to kick a field goal, which would put them up by 9. That would put the game out of reach. T-Lloyd and his teammates simply could not allow them to score.

T-Lloyd couldn't help but stare at the yellow uprights. After all, a field goal would pretty much end the game.

On first down, the ball was snapped and T-Lloyd pushed forward with all his might. The center placed his hands right above the "72" on T-Lloyd's jersey and gave him a hard push, knocking him back momentarily. Recovering, T-Lloyd noticed Daniel Pressman, the South Grand Prairie quarterback, dropping back to throw the ball. T-Lloyd thrust his left arm into the air just in time to deflect the pass off his fingertips. The ball fell harmlessly to the ground, stopping the clock. The Bell crowd jumped to its feet and cheered.

On second down, T-Lloyd had a hunch it was going to be a run. Pressman wouldn't want to take a chance on another incomplete pass, which would stop the clock again. T-Lloyd focused on the ball, preparing himself for a jarring collision with the offensive line. Then, just as he expected, Pressman handed the ball off to his running back.

Because T-Lloyd had been overpowering all game long, the center and another offensive lineman were *both* focused on him. One of them violently jabbed T-Lloyd in the ribs, while the other tried to knock him backward with a crushing blow. But T-Lloyd refused to back down. He lowered his left shoulder and hit right back, knocking *both* offensive linemen off-balance. Then he spun away from them, and with one free arm, reached out to try to make a tackle on the oncoming running back. T-Lloyd grabbed his ankle and held on tight. This slowed the running back down for a moment.

That's all it took. One of T-Lloyd's teammates, a big linebacker, rushed over and smothered the running back. It was a gain of only one yard! T-Lloyd had done his job again. Of course, he wouldn't get credit for the tackle, but as a nose guard, he was used to that. As he puts it, "Playing nose guard is not about stats. It's about *football*. It's about lining up across from the biggest guys on the field, banging heads, and seeing who the real men are."

Now, on third and nine, everybody in the stadium knew that a pass was coming. Coach Olivo relayed the defensive play call from the sideline. Middle linebackers Taniela Vake and K.C. Aharanawa would blitz right up the middle. In the huddle, Taniela looked right at T-Lloyd and said, "It's on you. You gotta hold up those two inside guys!"

The Bell defensive line prepares for the biggest play of the game.

T-Lloyd nodded. He understood the situation. It was up to him to occupy *two* blockers, leaving only one blocker to take on Taniela *and* K.C. If T-Lloyd did his job, one of them would have a chance to get to the quarterback before he could get rid of the ball.

By now, the fans were stomping their feet and yelling loudly in support of their team. Everybody in the stadium could feel the momentum of the game shifting. South Grand Prairie had the ball, a six-point lead, and they were threatening. If Bell could somehow turn them away, that might put T-Lloyd's team in a position to get the ball back and score a touchdown for the win.

Daniel Pressman lined up a few yards behind center, in shotgun formation. He had a running back to his right. When the ball was hiked, T-Lloyd exploded forward from his crouched stance. He had to make himself as wide as possible to take on the two blockers who were paying close attention to him. It wasn't easy, because they were *huge*. The center dug his hands into T-Lloyd's chest as the offensive guard attacked from an angle. They pounded him with everything they had, but T-Lloyd refused to go down.

It was a fascinating battle that played out in the span of just a few seconds. The three players fought to maintain their position. Using the last gasp of effort in his powerful body, T-Lloyd barreled into them with all his strength. One player fell to the ground, while the other struggled with T-Lloyd, trying to hold him off.

That was all Taniela and K.C. needed. Taniela charged straight through a hole created by the absence of the two linemen T-Lloyd was battling. He crashed into Daniel Pressman, who couldn't get rid of the ball. That sack resulted in a ten-yard loss. South Grand Prairie was too far away to even attempt a field goal. They would have to punt. T-Lloyd and his teammates had stopped them cold! Bell called their final timeout, ready to get the ball back with a final chance to win.

As T-Lloyd jogged off the field, he was so tired and beaten up that he could barely move. Grabbing a water bottle and sitting on one knee, he flipped off his helmet and sprayed cool water on his face.

The crowd was amped and so were the players. Momentum is a strange thing in sports. It can work for you or against you, but it's unquestionably a powerful thing. With the cheers of the crowd ringing in their ears, and the boost from their tremendous defensive series, the Blue Raiders suddenly caught fire. They steadily drove down the field, until they found themselves on the Warriors' 20-yard line with 15 seconds left to play.

Over on the sideline, T-Lloyd and his fellow defensive linemen were shouting encouragement to their teammates. That's what football is truly all about. "We're brothers," T-Lloyd explains. "Sure, we did our job on the defensive end, but that doesn't matter. We win or lose as a team."

It was third down and one. But because there was so little time left on the clock, a first down wouldn't help the Blue Raiders now. It was time to go for it all. Dropping back to pass, quarterback Logan Smith scrambled and looked for someone to throw to. He spotted one of his receivers, Atem Bol, who had curled and was now running straight to the end zone. Just before being hit by a blitzing linebacker, Logan fired a bullet. It was a little high, but Bol leaped up and made a spectacular catch in the end zone. The referees both raised their hands. Touchdown, Bell!

The noise was deafening. T-Lloyd, his teammates, and the huge crowd were screaming and celebrating. The extra point was good a moment later, capping off an unlikely 15-14 victory. Bell was going to the playoffs!

For T-Lloyd, this was a major achievement. As a senior, there was no next year for him at Bell. His time was *now*. It had been a tumultuous high school career for him: Hurricane *Katrina*, moving to a different state, new friends and teammates. But showing the same type of determination that was his trademark on the football field, T-Lloyd had adjusted, and even flourished.

Later on, in the locker room, reporters and local news crews were crowding around Logan Smith and Atem Bol, asking them about that last spectacular touchdown pass. As usual, the defensive linemen were not asked many questions.

All of a sudden, David Fisher, the coach of South Grand Prairie, walked in the locker room. First he offered congratulations to Coach Olivo. Then he made a special point of walking over to T-Lloyd's locker and extending his hand. "That was a heck of a game you played, son. I can't remember the last time I've seen a lineman dominate in the trenches the way you did out there today."

T-Lloyd was humbled by those words of praise. Guys who play on the line live for moments like these. They understand that the majority of people don't really think about them too much, because so much focus is placed on the "skill" positions, like quarterback, running back, and receiver. That's why there's no better feeling than an opposing coach complimenting you after the game.

T-Lloyd's high school career was winding down. But performances like this, and the recognition of an opposing coach, made him realize that he was playing the game the right way. All that hard work was paying off. He was feeling confident that he could take the next step and compete at the college level. It would be just one more challenge in a lifetime of challenges.

Chillin' in the pool: T-Lloyd's positive attitude continues to help him overcome obstacles and achieve great things on the football field, socially, and in the classroom.

CHAPTER EIGHT

T-LLOYD

Thomas Lloyd III, AKA T-Lloyd, has a lot to be proud about. He has faced—and overcome—many obstacles. He had to deal with the trauma of Hurricane *Katrina*. That alone is more than most kids ever go through. But it was just the beginning for him. Because of it, his family had to move to a new state and T-Lloyd had to switch schools right before his sophomore year of high school. It was a difficult time: adjusting to a new home, new friends, and of course, having to establish himself as a football player all over again on a new team.

During these trying times, T-Lloyd could have quit on his dreams. Instead, he became stronger. Through it all, he has never lost sight of his future. While he dreams of starring in the NFL, he also knows that the career of most NFL linemen isn't very long—about four seasons on average. That's because of all the pounding and physical abuse they have to endure.

So it hasn't been only football. Even with the practices, the games, and the early morning sessions in the weight room, T-Lloyd has kept up his grades. Actually, he's done a lot more than just keep them up. He has become an honors student at Bell, accumulating a 3.2 grade-point average.

T-Lloyd's inspired play on the defensive line, coupled with his fine grades, started raising eyebrows across the country. Many opportunities opened up for this talented senior. Several colleges got in touch with him, some offering him a full-ride scholarship to attend their university. T-Lloyd was on his way to becoming the first member of his family to graduate college!

T-Lloyd is a great example of someone who didn't neglect school just so he could play sports. "Sure, there are times that I'm tired from football or lifting weights," he says, putting down his math book. "But I have a long life ahead of me, whether or not I make the NFL. I want a career after my playing days are over. College is my ticket to that career."

T-Lloyd has his heart set on studying business and marketing. Along with his outgoing personality, a college degree will make him valuable to any team—and by "team" that could mean advertising agencies, business corporations, public relations firms, and many other types of companies.

Anyone who follows high school or college football is well aware of the significance of the first Wednesday in February each year. That day holds the fate of every college—and every high school senior—in the nation. It's known as "National Signing Day" for high school foot

T-Lloyd the businessman.

ball players. This is when most high school athletes sign an official letter to commit to the college of their choice.

In 2008, National Signing Day fell on Wednesday, February 6. That was shaping up to be the proudest, and also the most important day of T-Lloyd's life. He had a tough decision to make. After all the research and recruiting visits, he had three excellent schools to choose from: Fordham University, Abilene Christian University, and the Virginia Military Institute. They had each offered him a full scholarship.

These fine institutions all have quality business programs, so T-Lloyd knew he couldn't lose. Just as importantly, each of them has a well-regarded football program. That's where the decision became difficult. T-Lloyd has big dreams on the football field, so he needed to select a college team that would allow him to grow and continue to develop his skills.

Early in the morning on Wednesday, February 6, 2008, T-Lloyd set off a wild celebration in the Lloyd household by announcing his decision. In the end, after many weeks of careful deliberation, he had decided to attend Fordham University. His mother cried in happiness, and wouldn't stop hugging her giant son.

A small private school located in New York City, Fordham is a long way from Hurst, Texas. That's okay with T-Lloyd. College is all about embarking on new adventures. He has never lived anywhere besides Texas or Louisiana, but going to New York City will be a dream come true. Although being far away from his family is going to be tough, T-Lloyd is ready for the next chapter in his life.

While Fordham is considered a smaller-sized school by some, it's still a respected football university. It's a perfect place for T-Lloyd to play and continue to improve. Remember, he's only been playing nose tackle for a couple of years. Who can imagine how good he will be with more coaching and several years of NCAA experience?

A building at Fordham University.

Fordham University has a storied past, including many players who have gone on to play in the NFL. The most famous graduate of FU is the legendary coach mentioned in the first chapter of this book: Vince Lombardi, class of 1937.

Lombardi would later go on to coach the Green Bay Packers and turn them into a powerhouse. Prior to his arrival, the Packers hadn't enjoyed a winning season in ten years. Lombardi changed all that. He led them to *five* NFL championships. His influence in the NFL was so great that, after retiring, he was given a tremendous honor. Each year, the team that wins the Super Bowl is awarded a trophy. It's what every NFL team shoots for: The *Vince Lombardi* Trophy.

T-Lloyd hopes that one day he will be another Fordham graduate who goes on to do great things in the NFL. However, his dreams don't end there. As his weightlifting improved dramatically, his interest in it continued to grow. T-Lloyd decided to take it to the next level. He joined the Bell power lifting squad and also began competing around Texas. His accomplishments are truly impressive. He has squatted 550 pounds and bench-pressed 360 pounds! By his senior year, he found himself ranked in the top 10 in the Dallas/Fort Worth area.

With such tremendous improvement, T-Lloyd would like to take weightlifting to the highest level in the world: the Olympics.

It's ironic, because there is no football competition in the Olympics, but of course there is for weightlifting. It's good that he avoided steroids and all the other illegal substances that some athletes use.

Whether or not T-Lloyd ends up competing in the Olympics, in the NFL, or in the business world, he has charted a clear course for success in his life. His love of football might have been the starting point, but more than anything, it was all about enthusiasm, energy, and effort.

It makes a lot of sense that T-Lloyd is a nose tackle. In many ways, it fits his personality. While other players get more glory and headlines, he's the one in the trenches doing his job to help his team win. That's what he's all about. It is this type of attitude and maturity that has served him well so far.

New Orleans, Texas, and now Fordham University—all of them will be better places because they were blessed with the presence of a huge kid with an even bigger heart. T-Lloyd always seems to have a big smile on his face. So if you ever see him at the stadium, or even just walking down the street, be sure to say hello. He was born Thomas Lloyd III. His family calls him T.J. But to anybody else who comes into contact with him, or is lucky enough to call him a teammate, classmate, or friend ... he's just T-Lloyd.

In the trenches, it's all about heart.
How big is yours?